Stay Conscious: Inside Black America's Mind

By Iriel Hampton

JD Publishing, 2015

ISBN 978-1505892659

Contents

Introduction

Origins of the System at Hand: Birth of Black America

Equity, Equality, and Freedom: The Development of Black America

The Current State of Black America: Stagnation

Charge for Change: Advancement

A Collection of Conscious Writings:

I Can't Breathe

Letter to Black Women

What does it mean to be African American: Uproar in our Beloved Country

Afterword

About the Author

Introduction

Are you conscious of the current state of Black America? She holds more secrets than truths. Black America is bleeding with the tears of weeping mothers. She makes a strong outcry for justice, strength, stability, assurance, and faith. Yet, she is fed with self-hatred and fueled by the need to conform to "societal norms." Right and wrong are only subjective ideals of a society not created for Black America, but for a broken system born out of greed. You are conscious of the losses Black America has seen, but are you staying conscious? We tend to forget about Black America after her sorrows have crept into the past. Individualism creates a crisis. When sorrows subside, history repeats itself because the immediate present forgot to amend the problem. We should be conscious of the origin of the system, the true definition of equality, and what needs to change in Black America.

Origins of the System at Hand:

Birth of Black America

It is human nature to desire riches; this same desire has broken nature. Humanity has sold himself for the temporary capital gains of the world. A group of people can be controlled when another group determines their differences and capitalizes on them. Black America was birthed a nation enslaved, bogged down by the chains of her differences. Willie Lynch, a plantation owner from the West Indies, outlined these differences in 1712 when he delivered the speech: *The Making of A Slave,* to the Colony of Virginia. He states, "You must pitch the OLD black male vs. the YOUNG black male, and the YOUNG black male against the OLD black male. You must use the DARK skin slaves vs. the LIGHT skin slaves, and the LIGHT skin slaves vs. the DARK skin slaves. You must use the FEMALE vs. the MALE, and the MALE vs. the FEMALE." We are conscious of these differences, but are we not conscious of society's role in controlling these differences? Lynch advises to break the female slave so that she reverses the gender roles of her offspring. She shall train her son to be mentally dependent and weak but physically strong, while training her female offspring to be psychologically independent. This process kills the "protective male image." He goes on to advise creating an illusion of societal hierarchy by placing slaves with lighter skin

7

in a less labor intensive position on the plantation. With this system, envy will outweigh admiration and distrust will be stronger than trust. Does this sound familiar? The origins of the problems in Black America were not formed by Black America. Yet, Black America is constantly blamed for a cycle forced upon her during the bonds of enslavement. We must be sure to know and remember our history. Lynch warns that this process can be reversed by knowledge. Knowledge reverses illusion. The human brain reverts back to the natural order of society, but only if a child is reared with historical knowledge.

Education is not at the forefront of Black America's concerns. We are still concerned with riches; the same element that broke our ancestors down and allowed us to sell our people into slavery. If one has an adequate education, he can rise up the socioeconomic ladder. Be cognitive of the fact that Black America's lower educational values do not stem from Black America herself, but from societal pressures of reconstruction after the Civil War. Students learn from teachers and teachers teach what is placed in the state curriculum with resources provided by the state. Education does not only encompass what the state wants a student to learn, but what parents teach their children at home. If a mother or father is well educated and stays conscious of the injustices and framework of society, then their offspring has a better chance of defying all norms by working through society's oppressive systematics. The initial, free public education system after the Civil War embodied inequality. History was not written from the slave's point of view. Emphasis was placed on what was important to the majority of America. Black America never had the option of creating her own educational system. People like Maya Angelou and Dr. W.E.B. DuBois strived to correct the perspective of history, and wrote books through the lens of Black America. The resources are there, but what percentage of Black America is conscious of or exposed to writings as such?

Equity, Equality, and

Freedom:

The Development of Black

America

Equality is defined as "the state of being equal in status, rights, and opportunities." Society pushes for hard work. Hard work should allow one to have the same status, rights, and opportunities of the most successful people in America. This flawed misconception forces Black America to walk before she can even envision crawling. The emphasis of hard work would hold validity if equality did not also encompass the power of government exclusion. A person without societal privilege can work hard their entire life and never be on the same footing as those of the privileged majority. Thus, Black America must define equality on her own terms. Black America encompasses her own identity. The only success that can arise from a system of this sort is individual success of a particular subset of African Americans. These individuals become immersed in a culture with ideals that are not their own and may even hold the same twisted concepts of societal equality. Individual success excludes the remaining population of Black America. Black America can never succeed as a whole if she continues to allow an individualistic conception of societal equality grasp her people.

Equity can be defined as "a justice to natural law or right." This is where Black America's idealism of equality should lie. The idea of equity allows Black America to crawl. Black

America is full of different types of people, different temperaments, and different learning styles. The idea is that people begin life at different stages with no fault or effort to begin in such place. Because people begin in different stages, they are not to be treated as they are at the same stage. Talents are not being nourished, resulting in the slow shrivel of Black America's potential to succeed.

Freedom commences when people realize the true definition of equality. Is Black America truly free, or does she only believe she's free because American society says that freedom is individualism? Power lies within the law and the people who dictate those laws control freedom. Black America gained power the day she gained suffrage. You are conscious of your right to vote, but are you staying conscious? You have the power to vote for judges, senators and laws which is everything this society considers justice. In 2012, the Black American voter turnout stood at an all-time high when 66.2% of eligible voters utilized their right to cast ballots. This huge turnout helped tremendously in President Barack Obama's re-election. It is clear that Black America has power, but the presidential election is not the only time voting should matter. Local elections and state elections matter just as much as the presidential elections. All voting should matter including the primaries. Both Congress and the Senate vote for laws, this is the same on a state level. You can control what is happening around you. Black America holds so much power, yet she

12

forgets to utilize her strengths. Please do not forget to stay conscious for this will enable us to walk.

The Current State of Black

America: Stagnation

Family structure is the root of all fruitful communities. Black America is in conflict with societal family structure and her own determined family structure. Because of the origin of the system at hand, Black Americans are not taught how to be a mate or how to work with the opposite sex. Women are taught to be strong, because of their origins. With this system, families tend to grow as single parent homes. Three generations of women arise and those women only know what they have been taught and what they've seen. Women have been taught to be independent and strong since the birth of Black America. Society does not teach women to be strong and independent. Society says that the man is the breadwinner and the woman is the caregiver. Do you see the problem here? Black America continuously strives to reach the accepted societal norms only when Black America does not belong in that societal norm therefore causing the family structure to be broken. We must learn how to define our own societal norms and make the family structure work. Take responsibility for your family. Your family is a reflection of you and you are a reflection of the community. Instill the importance of education in your children and nourish their talents. Men, remember that you are a role model no matter if the young man looking up to you is your son or not. Boys grow into who they want to be, men show them who they want to be. Ask yourself, are you the man you would want a young boy to model himself after? With the lack of community role models, youth tend to look to the media instead. However, the media is biased. Media says that the average criminal is a Black Man. Media creates the illusion of an unhealthy culture. The media makes Black American culture seem so horrible that men like Michael Dunn say things such as, "I'm really not prejudiced against race, but I have no use for certain cultures. This gangster-rap, ghetto talking thug 'culture' that certain segments of society flock to is intolerable. They espouse violence and disrespect towards women. The black community here in Jacksonville is in an uproar against me -- the 3 other thugs that were in the car are telling stories to cover up their true colors." Adult men start thinking that it is okay to kill Black America's young boys because they are afraid of a culture implanted in their minds by the media. Is media really an accurate source for youth to follow? When you define your own societal norm, share that with your son. Show him how you treat a woman and he will treat his own daughter and wife that way. Be cognitive of the fact that your culture is beautiful. Think about who created a negative outlook on Black Culture. The words we allow society to use with negative connotations such as "ghetto" and "ratchet" have caused our own people to stray away from the culture, and to race to individualistic success. This is the reason Black America cries. If she hates herself, who can love her?

Black owned businesses and colleges exist, but who is utilizing them? Society says that these businesses and universities are inadequate compared to their similar counterparts. When you hear "Ivy League University" what immediately comes to mind? Academic competition, selectivity, elitism, and athletic prowess are just a few thoughts to say the least. Yet, when someone mentions "Historically Black Colleges" none of those adjectives make an appearance in Black America's mind. Students turn their nose up at the idea of attending a school that has lost its accreditation just a few years prior to them considering enrollment. Yet, they don't understand that these very schools may have just lost funding because our own people are not supporting them. Universities such as Howard University, Hampton University, Xavier University, Morehouse College, and Spellman College uphold high standards and produce EXCELLENT graduates who are constantly changing the world. These colleges nourish students and encourage them to be successful even though they may not have originally considered attending college. Despite the numerous track records of success, the majority of black students do not have a Historically Black College or University as a top choice when filling out college applications. The first step for Historically Black Colleges to gain ground and rise among the elite in the 21st century where society is pushing for inclusion, is to redefine Black America's mind. The stereotype of an inadequate school or business exists because Black America does not support herself. She depends on faulty origins and a society that does not care about her as a collective whole.

"Tertium quid" is the term Dr. W.E.B. DuBois used to define society's view of Black America in *Souls of Black Folk*. "Tertium quid" describes a third element in between two known elements. This is what Black America has allowed society to define her as because she is not the majority culture. African Americans are coined "tertium quid" which is a being between man and animal. As defined by the majority culture, we have been so far displaced from beauty that instead we are defined as inhumane creatures. Create your own definition of beauty, force society to love you for your standard of beauty, not vice versa. Erase the lines of skin color bias that exists in Black America. The bias that says, "those that are closer to the majority culture are closer to beauty." Everyone holds beauty, no matter what shade.

Charge for Change:

Advancement

"We must raise serious and basic questions about the overall role played by federal funds in relation to the black liberation struggle. Our basic premise is that money and jobs are not the final answer to the black man's problems. Without, in any sense, denying the overwhelming reality of poverty, we must affirm that the basic goal is not 'welfare colonialism,' as some have called the anti-poverty and other federal programs, but the inclusion of black people at all levels of decision-making. We do not seek to be mere recipients *from* the decision-making process but participants *in* it." *–Black Power: The Politics of Liberation by Kwame Ture and Charles V. Hamilton.* Seek to participate in the decisions made for Black America. Be her representative through voting in, not only presidential elections, but local elections as well. Strive to be senators, government officials, and business owners. Black America has the potential to be powerful. The power is there, we just need to utilize it. Educators, send your best students to Historically Black Colleges. Parents, work to stay together and be role models for your children. Love your culture, love who you are. When you realize your talents, use them to better Black America. Do not fall into a trap of individualism. Do not focus on failure or flaws because Black America and the world may never see something that could have made a change. "The more I focus less on myself, the more I realize I can be used to spread a message" –*Erykah Badu*. We all have a purpose in life. Embrace yours, never forget your origins, and stay conscious of the system at hand.

Do not allow sorrows to subside, for if history repeats itself, Black America's future will surely go down a gloomy path. Transform individualism into collectivism. Redefine Black America. You are conscious of the potential Black America holds, but are you staying conscious? Explain to society why Black America is powerful. Embrace yourself, you are what you are. As you would feed your offspring, feed Black America with love, not self-hatred. Create "black societal norms." Do not ignore her outcry for justice, strength, stability, assurance and faith. Black America's bleeding wounds should be healed by her own people. Allow the world to hear her truths. Are you conscious of the current state of Black America? You are now, stay conscious.

A Collection of Conscious Writings

I Can't Breathe

I Can't Breathe
Breath

Breath (noun)

\ˈbreth\

•The basic motion we as human beings need to perform.

•The inspiration and expulsion of oxygen to and from the
lungs.

•That feeling of satisfaction after our bodies obtain air;

•That notion that we need not worry because air, as abundant
as it is, will always be there.

High income, low income, we all desire and long to take… a
breath.

We are all intertwined through the connectivity of this
socialization called humanity. Yet, we capitalize on our
differences.

How silly would it be to begin charging for air? Competitive
companies would arise, benefiting from the financial gains of
taking a breath. It would result in a system where the wealthy
would get to determine what is done with air, how much
oxygen one can obtain in a cubic inch of air, and the shaming
of people who did not have the time or resources to hop on
the train of "let's make a profit from inhalation of air." Let's add
the fact that laws are created by the people who were able to

24

hop on that train, restricting factions of society that are different from obtaining this basic human right. Low income, the uninformed, "outsiders," and anyone left out of the quest for capitalization of basic needs would not be able to sustain life. But wait, there is an exception. There may be a few people who want workers in their air purification plants. They can get paid enough just to obtain the sufficient amount of air to survive. A union may arise, demanding higher quality air for workers. The government may step in and give them pensions for air (nowhere near enough for comfortable breathing quality of course). All the while, the wealthy are blaming the workers for their misfortunes, and bashing the government for giving out pensions. Maybe if the workers worked harder in life they would have better quality air. The humanity has left all factions of this scenario. The scenario sounds absurd and outrageous. Everyone has the right to air…right? Everyone has the right to live.

What about food? Is food something we all need as human beings to survive?

What about shelter? On a societal level, is shelter something we need to survive?

What about equality? On a psychological level, what does this do to the mind?

How is the psych affected when you are born into a society where you are denied basic human rights because you are different?

No matter how outrageous this scenario seems, it's our reality.

Wake up, take a breath, and take a look at what you stand for.

-Iriel Hampton

Letter from the Black Woman:

My Sister's Keeper?

Letter from the Black Woman: My Sister's Keeper?

To my sisters,

Do you feel that your joy is negated when walking into a room full of black sisters? What does it mean to keep your sister? **I am a woman....and I am black.** That means that when I speak or wear modern clothing I can easily be conveyed by society as excessively aggressive and overly sexualized. I must make a conscious decision every morning to make sure that not only am I aware of my presence in society but that I am also aware of my black sister's perception of me. Why? My black sisters tear me down. My black sisters see success and wonder where it came from. My black sisters see my flaws and indulge in ridicule. **My black sisters see me with the man they desire and hate me.** My black sisters fight each other on *WorldStar* and make our disagreements a public spectacle. My black sisters look down upon my natural hair and my decision to embrace my natural beauty. My black sisters bully me emotionally and form cliques in order to shape their identity while leaving me to find my own. **I am a black woman and I am alone.** Who is for me when my own sisters are against me? I desire to see a world where black women see one another succeed and hop on that glory; see that we can help one another succeed. **I want to see black women help one another when they see a flaw instead of teasing and immersing their sisters in a pool of ridicule. I need that sister to take that correction and better herself.** I want black women to keep one another as close to their hearts as they keep their values and **love**. I want black women to join together, **reach back, move forward,** and bring other sisters with them. When my sister makes progress, I am happy. I wish for us to be each other's keeper; learn from each other, correct each other, and uplift one another.

-Iriel Hampton

What does it mean to be

African American:

Uproar in our Beloved

Country

"I'm tired of being labeled. I'm an American. I'm not an African American; I'm an American." -Raven-Symone

African American social media users went into an uproar over Raven-Symone's declaration to the world about her decision not to identify herself as an African American on Oprah Winfrey's Network. This comment brought up the further discussion of why people in America are so uncomfortable with discussing race. Place all of this uproar with the arrest of Dr. Cornel West in Ferguson, Missouri and you will find yourself in the most uncomfortable battle of morality, identity, and civic unrest all resulting from being, not only American, but African American in our beloved country.

It is important to remember that while refusing a label, you are refusing years of history. It is also important to remember that your refusal of that label will not stop society from labeling you as such.

What does it mean to be African American?

Being African American means to be Black in America. The only negative connotation that it receives comes from society, and Black Americans ashamed of their own culture. It means being the ambassador or pioneer of a generation that has matriculated an ongoing struggle of assimilation by force and by perceived need. It means holding a unique culture and history not everyone can understand. Rather than being lost in a melting pot, African Americans are the fruits in America's "fruit salad." America loves African American culture, including dances and colloquialisms. Identity should not be in question; however, both identity and morality are in question as bystanders watch the civic unrest in Ferguson, Missouri. Questions arise such as, "Why is this happening to those that look like me?" and "What can I do?" Maybe you do want to do something, but don't want to interrupt your day to day life. Either you embrace the label and do something for those like you, or you alienate yourself and stay away from the race discussions.

-Iriel Hampton

Afterword

My intention is to get readers to start thinking about how they can redefine the mind of Black America. Definition starts from within. We have continuously let outside forces define who we are. Remember that you are the master of your fate and the captain of your soul. You are Black America, her soul lives within you. Stay Conscious.

About the Author

From the moment I first stepped foot on my college campus, I knew it would be an entirely new ball game. I made the conscious decision to give back to my community because I knew that I had reached a place that many young adults don't even get the chance to experience. It was then that I decided to find a non-profit company that helps educate children. I looked to the organization entitled *Austin Partners In Education*. In Texas, the format of standardized testing took a huge turn. The TAKS test was not timed but the new STARR test only gave students an allotted amount of time for each section and contained more complex problems. For two years, I worked alongside *Austin Partners in Education* tutoring students from grades 6-8 in preparation for the math portion of the STARR test. While working in a school setting, I noticed how some students were bullied and obviously from different social backgrounds than others. This observation inspired me to seek a mentee. With *Big Brothers, Big Sisters of America,* I mentored a nine year old girl named Connie who absolutely admired me. I met with her twice a month and traveled with her to places like the library and the park. She created a scrapbook of our many adventures. I loved doing activities for both the community and on campus. During my freshman year of college, I also joined the *African American Culture Committee (AACC)*. AACC held forums and events throughout the semester that uplifted the black community.

We brought a number of motivational speakers like Brian White to campus, collected donations for breast cancer research, and held forums to teach students how to study effectively. I also participated in the "Miss Quintessential" Scholarship Pageant held by the men of Omega Psi Phi Fraternity, Inc. During preparation of the pageant, I learned the importance of perseverance, time management, and self-discipline. A portion of the money collected from the pageant went to refurbish damaged books in low-income schools. As a strong believer of paying it forward and sharing life lessons, I began to work as a college recruitment counselor at Arlington Heights High School in order to help instill the value of education, perseverance, time management, and self-discipline into young minds. Before long, another opportunity arose for me to step up and become the president of the *University Democrats* my very first semester of transferring to a new and unfamiliar campus. I took on the vigorous role and begin to work with companies to get President Obama re-elected. Organization members dedicated their time by volunteering at call centers with the goal of informing Florida democrats of their respective poll locations and reminding them to vote. When President Obama was re-elected, I know it was the youth who helped make a difference. With their help, we were also able to get Congressman Marc Veasey on campus to speak about turning the state of Texas blue. During this same time, I also joined the *National Association* for the Advancement of Colored People (NAACP) and the National Association for Colored Woman's Club (NACWC). Both organizations stressed the importance of community service. My chapter of NAACP participates in bi-monthly trips to the Boys and Girls Club to tutor and mentor the youth. We also participate in Habitat for Humanity with the goal of preserving a home every year. We have held political forums to stress the importance of midterm elections and a formal discussion of what Dr. Martin Luther King Jr. would do if he were here with us today in the community. During elections, we helped organize a group of members to march to the polls and vote together. We also held an AIDS awareness day to help educate members of society on what is now our reality in the HIV/AIDS fight. I realize that NAACP has created a huge legacy, one in which the college units should follow. I also became a member of Delta Sigma Theta Sorority Inc. my junior year of college. My chapter has donated to St. Jude's Children Research Hospital which is a continued legacy as of this year. We strive to educate the campus community about finances, business, the importance of education and community service. I am the former 1st Vice President of the UT Arlington chapter of NAACP where our motto is, "Be the Change." Creating and editing The Black Maverick for UT Arlington's Center for African American Studies gives me an outlet to "Be the Change." In every task of life, I strive to change the situations I believe are unjust, and let every decision have purpose.